CATS
SET II

American Curl Cats

Stuart A. Kallen
ABDO & Daughters

visit us at
www.abdopub.com

Published by Abdo & Daughters, 4940 Viking Drive, Suite 622, Edina, Minnesota 55435.
Copyright © 1998 by Abdo Consulting Group, Inc., Pentagon Tower, P.O. Box 36036,
Minneapolis, Minnesota 55435 USA. International copyrights reserved in all countries.
No part of this book may be reproduced in any form without written permission from the
publisher.

Printed in the United States.

Photo credits: Peter Arnold, Inc., Animals Animals, TICA

Edited by Lori Kinstad Pupeza

Library of Congress Cataloging-in-Publication Data

Kallen, Stuart A., 1955-
     American curl cats / by Stuart A. Kallen.
     p. cm. -- (Cats. Set II)
     Includes index.
     Summary: Presents information about the breed of cat that was discovered in
California in 1981 and whose ear tips are curved back and towards the center of
its head.
     ISBN 1-56239-578-5
     1. American curl cat--Juvenile literature. [1. American curl cat. 2. Cats.] I.
Title. II. Series: Kallen, Stuart A., 1955- Cats. Set II.
     SF449.A44K34 1998
     636.8'3--dc20

                                                               95-52344
                                                               CIP
                                                               AC

Contents

Lions, Tigers, and Cats

Few animals are as beautiful and graceful as cats. And all cats are related. From the wild lions of Africa to common house cats, all belong to the family **Felidae**. Wild cats are found almost everywhere. They include cheetahs, jaguars, lynx, ocelots, and **domestic** cats.

Cats were first domesticated around 5,000 years ago in the Middle East.

Even though tamed house cats don't look like the wild beasts that roam through the wilderness, they do have a lot in common. All cats move the same way. They walk on their toes and leap and bound after their prey. This makes all cats great hunters.

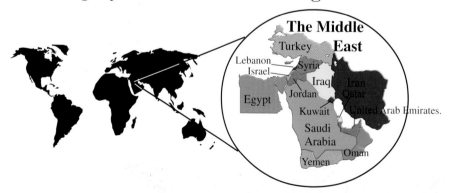

The Middle East

Turkey
Lebanon
Israel
Syria
Iraq
Iran
Egypt
Jordan
Qatar
Kuwait
United Arab Emirates.
Saudi
Arabia
Oman
Yemen

All cats are related to each other.

American Curls

The American curl cat has ear tips that are curved back and towards the center of its head. The first American curl was discovered in California in 1981 by Joe and Grace Ruga. The Rugas found a black, longhaired stray outside their home. The cat had curled ears.

When the Rugas bred the cat with another normal cat, two of the kittens had the curled ears. The cats were displayed at shows and were a hit with cat lovers. American curls became an **official breed** in 1983.

Opposite page: An American curl cat.

Qualities

American curls are playful, healthy cats. They are curious and fun-loving. Because they were first bred from stray cats, these cats make good mouse catchers. They are gentle with children and get along well with other cats.

American curls are intelligent and charming. Like any cat, the American curl cat likes to play games. It will pounce and attack anything in its view.

Opposite page: American curls are intelligent and charming.

Coat and Color

American curls are bred in long and shorthair types. Longhaired curls should have silky coats of medium length. Shorthaired curls should have smooth, short, and silky coats.

American curl cats may be any color, including black, white, brown, and blue-gray. Curls may be spotted or have tabby markings. Some curls even have markings like Siamese cats.

Opposite page: A longhaired American curl.

Size

American curls are medium-sized cats who weigh between 5 and 10 pounds (2 to 4.5 kg). They have muscular bodies and medium-thick legs with rounded paws. Their hind legs are slightly longer in back than in the front.

Their plumed tails are wide at the base and thinner at the tip. American curls have soft ears that curl back and inward. They have tufts of fur on the tips of their ears.

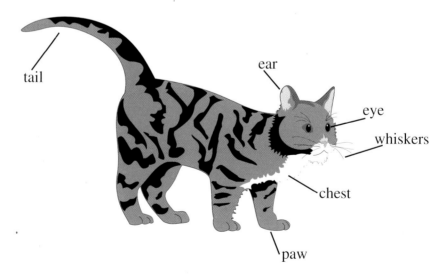

American curls
are medium-sized cats.

Care

American curls are friendly and gentle. Longhaired types need a good brushing at least once a week. Besides making the cat purr, this will keep its loose hair off of furniture.

Like any pet, an American curl needs a lot of love and attention. Cats make fine pets. But American curls still have some of their wild instincts. Cats are natural hunters and like to explore outdoors.

A **scratching post** where the cat can sharpen its claws saves furniture from damage. A cat buries its waste and should be trained to use a litter box. The box needs to be cleaned every day. American curls love to play. A ball, **catnip**, or a loose string will keep a kitten busy for hours.

Cats should be **neutered** or **spayed**. Females can have dozens of kittens in a year. Males will spray very unpleasant odors indoors and out if not fixed.

American curls love to play.

Feeding

Cats are meat eaters. Hard bones that do not splinter help keep cats' teeth and mouths clean. If a cat lives outside, it will hunt for birds or rodents. It will provide for itself with a good diet.

Most cats live indoors. Water should always be available. Most cats survive fine on dried cat food. They like **catnip** and other treats. Although they love milk, it often causes cats to become ill.

Opposite page: Cats are natural hunters.

Kittens

A female cat is pregnant for about 65 days. When kittens are born, there may be from two to eight babies. The average cat has four kittens. Kittens are blind and helpless for the first few weeks.

After about three weeks they will start crawling and playing. At this time they may be given cat food. After about a month, kittens will run, wrestle, and play games. If the cat is a **pedigree**, it should be **registered** and given papers at this time. At 10 weeks the kittens are old enough to be sold or given away.

About half of American curl kittens will have curved ears. But when they are born, their ears will look normal. The changes will be noticed in about five to seven days. The curl develops for about six months.

Only about half of American curl kittens
will have curved ears.

Buying a Kitten

The best place to get an American curl is from a breeder. Cat shows are also good places to find kittens. Next you must decide if you want a simple pet or a show winner. A basic American curl cat can cost $50. A blue-ribbon winner can cost as much as $300. When you buy an American curl, you should get **pedigree** papers that **register** the animal with the **Cat Fanciers Association**.

When buying a kitten, check it closely for signs of good health. The ears, nose, mouth, and fur should be clean. Eyes should be bright and clear. The cat should be alert and interested in what is going on around it. A healthy kitten will move around with its head held high.

Opposite page: A pure bred
American curl can cost $300.

21

Glossary

breed/official breed - a kind of cat, an American curl is a breed of cat. An official breed is a breed that is recognized by special cat organizations.

Cat Fanciers Association - a group that sets the standards for the breeds of cats.

catnip - the dried leaves and stems of a plant of the mint family, used as a stuffing for cats' toys because cats are stimulated by and drawn to its strong smell.

domestic/domesticated - tamed or adapted to home life.

Felidae - Latin name given to the cat family.

neutered - a male cat that is neutered cannot get a female cat pregnant.

non-pedigree - an animal without a record of its ancestors.

pedigree - a record of an animal's ancestors.

register - to add a cat to an official list of its breed.

scratching post - a post for a cat to scratch on, which is usually made out of wood or covered with carpet, so the cat can wear down its nails.

spayed - a female cat that is spayed cannot have kittens.

Internet Sites

All About Cats
http://w3.one.net/~mich/index.html
See pictures of cats around the net, take a cat quiz to win prizes, and there is even a cat advice column. This is a fun and lively site.

Cat Fanciers Website
http://www.fanciers.com/
Information on breeds, shows, genetics, breed rescue, catteries and other topics. This is a very informative site, including clubs and many links.

Cats Homepage
http://www.cisea.it/pages/gatto/meow.htm
Page for all cat lovers. Cat photo gallery, books and more. This site has music and chat rooms, it's a lot of fun.

Cats Cats Cats
http://www.geocities.com/Heartland/Hills/5157/
This is just a fun site with pictures of cats, links, stories, and other cat stuff.

These sites are subject to change. Go to your favorite search engine and type in CATS for more sites.

PASS IT ON
Tell Others Something Special About Your Pet
To educate readers around the country, pass on interesting tips about animals, maybe a fun story about your animal or pet, and little unknown facts about animals. We want to hear from you!
To get posted on ABDO & Daughters website, E-mail us at "animals@abdopub.com"

Index